UNSPEAKABLE

Facing Up to Evil in
an Age of Genocide and Terror

OS GUINNESS

HarperSanFrancisco
A Division of HarperCollins*Publishers*

HarperCollins books may be purchased for educational, business, or sales promotional use. For information please write: Special Markets Department, HarperCollins Publishers, Inc., 10 East 53rd Street, New York, NY 10022.

HarperCollins Web site: http://www.harpercollins.com

HarperCollins®, ☷®, and HarperSanFrancisco™ are trademarks of HarperCollins Publishers, Inc.

Chapters 10, 11, and 12 contain material that was first published in *Long Journey Home: A Guide to Your Search for the Meaning of Life* (Colorado Springs, Colo.: WaterBrook Press; New York: Doubleday, 2001) and is used here with the publisher's permission.

FIRST EDITION

Library of Congress Cataloging-in-Publication Data
Guinness, Os
    Unspeakable : facing up to evil in an age of genocide and terror /
Os Guinness.—1st ed.
        p.   cm.
    Includes bibliographical references.
    ISBN 0-06-058636-2 (cloth)
    1. Good and evil. 2. Good and evil—Religious aspects—Christianity.
I. Title.
BJ1401.G85   2005
170—dc22   2004054032

05 06 07 08 09 ❖/RRD(H) 10 9 8 7 6 5 4 3 2 1

DOM
and to CJ,
and all in your generation
who have a passion to seek justice
and the courage to take a stand for it.